Diggers

Written by
Cath Jones

This is Jan. This is her job.

This is Dan. This is his job as well.

Jan and Dan sit with a helmet and a jacket on.

3

Digger Jobs

Chug! Chug!

Diggers can fix lots of big jobs. They can go in the mud.

This digger has a big bucket.

The bucket gets the mud.

Diggers can get manure with the bucket.

This digger has lots of manure in it.

This digger is a tipper.
It can tip up the mud.

This digger has a big magnet. The magnet hangs under the digger.

The magnet can pick up metal.

This digger has a big hammer. The digger hits the rocks with the big hammer.

Bash! Bash!

This man is a logger.
He gets logs with his digger.

This digger is a bit of a mess.

The digger man will go to the digger shop. Then he will get a much better digger.

Top jobs, diggers!